DØ952813

THE DIP

THE DIP

A LITTLE BOOK THAT TEACHES YOU
WHEN TO QUIT (AND WHEN TO STICK)

Seth Godin

Illustrated by Hugh Macleod

PORTFOLIO

PORTFOLIO
Published by the Penguin Group
Penguin Group (USA) Inc., 375 Hudson Street, New York, New York 10014,
U.S.A. • Penguin Group (Canada), 90 Eglinton Avenue East, Suite 700, Toronto,
Ontario, Canada M4P 2Y3 • (a division of Pearson Penguin Canada Inc.) •
Penguin Books Ltd., 80 Strand, London WC2R 0RL, England • Penguin
Ireland, 25 St. Stephen's Green, Dublin 2, Ireland (a division of Penguin Books
Ltd) • Penguin Books Australia Ltd, 250 Camberwell Road, Camberwell,
Victoria 3124, Australia • (a division of Pearson Australia Group Pty Ltd) •
Penguin Books India Pvt Ltd, 11 Community Centre, Panchsheel Park, New
Delhi – 110 017, India • Penguin Group (NZ), 67 Apollo Drive, Mairangi Bay,
Auckland 1311, New Zealand (a division of Pearson New Zealand Ltd.) •
Penguin Books (South Africa) (Pty) Ltd, 24 Sturdee Avenue, Rosebank,
Johannesburg 2196, South Africa

Penguin Books Ltd, Registered Offices: 80 Strand, London WC2R 0RL,
England

First published in 2007 by Portfolio, a member of Penguin Group (USA) Inc.

30

Copyright © Do You Zoom, Inc., 2007
All rights reserved

Illustrations by Hugh MacLeod

LIBRARY OF CONGRESS CATALOGING IN PUBLICATION DATA
Godin, Seth.
   The dip : a little book that teaches you when to quit (and when to stick) /
Seth Godin ; illustrated by Hugh Macleod.
      p.   cm.
   Includes bibliographical references and index.
   ISBN 978-1-59184-166-1
   1. Self-actualization (Psychology). 2. Success. 3. Success in business.
4. Persistence. I. Title.
   BF637.S4G63 2007
   158.1—dc22   2006036366

Printed in the United States of America
Set in Janson Text with Berthold Akzidenz Grotesk
Designed by Daniel Lagin

For Helene

THE DIP

Being the Best in the World Is Seriously Underrated

I FEEL LIKE GIVING UP.

Almost every day, in fact. Not all day, of course, but there are moments.

My bet is that you have those moments, too. If you're the kind of high-achieving, goal-oriented person who finds herself reading a book like this, you're probably used to running into obstacles. Professional obstacles, personal obstacles, even obstacles related to personal fitness or winning board games.

Most of the time, we deal with the obstacles by persevering. Sometimes we get discouraged and turn to inspirational writing, like stuff from Vince Lombardi: "Quitters never win and winners never quit." Bad advice. Winners quit all the time. *They just quit the right stuff at the right time.*

Most people quit. They just don't quit successfully. In fact, many professions and many marketplaces profit from quitters—society assumes you're going to quit. In fact, businesses and organizations count on it.

If you learn about the systems that have been put in place that encourage quitting, you'll be more likely to beat them. And once you understand the common sinkhole that trips up so many people (I call it the Dip), you'll be one step closer to getting through it.

Extraordinary benefits accrue to the tiny minority of people who are able to push just a tiny bit longer than most.

Extraordinary benefits also accrue to the tiny majority with the guts to quit early and refocus their efforts on something new.

In both cases, it's about being the best in the world. About getting through the hard stuff and coming out on the other side.

Quit the wrong stuff.
Stick with the right stuff.
Have the guts to do one or the other.

The Best in the World

Hannah Smith is a very lucky woman. She's a law clerk at the Supreme Court. She's the best in the world.

Last year, more than forty-two thousand people graduated from law school in the United States. And thirty-seven of them were awarded Supreme Court clerkships.

Those thirty-seven people are essentially guaranteed a job for life after they finish their year with the Court. Top law firms routinely pay a signing bonus of $200,000 or more to any clerk they are able to hire. Clerks go on to become partners, judges, and senators.

There are two things worth noting here. The first is that Hannah Smith isn't lucky at all. She's smart and focused and incredibly hardworking.

And the second thing? That any one of the forty-two thousand people who graduated from law school last year could have had Hannah's job. Except they didn't. Not because they weren't smart enough or because they came from the wrong family. No, the reason that most of them didn't have a chance is that somewhere along the way they quit. They didn't quit high school or college or law school. Instead, they quit in their quest to be the best in the world because the cost just seemed too high.

This is a very short book about a very important topic: quitting. Believe it or not, quitting is often a great strategy, a smart way to manage your life and your career. Sometimes, though, quitting is exactly the wrong thing to do. It turns out that there's a pretty simple way to tell the difference.

In addition to being smart and focused and incredibly

hardworking, Hannah Smith is also a quitter. In order to get as far as she's gotten, she's quit countless other pursuits. You really can't try to do everything, especially if you intend to be the best in the world.

Before we start on the quitting, though, you probably need to be sold on why being the best in the world matters so much.

The Surprising Value of Being the Best in the World

Our culture celebrates superstars. We reward the product or the song or the organization or the employee that is number one. The rewards are heavily skewed, so much so that it's typical for #1 to get ten times the benefit of #10, and a hundred times the benefit of #100.

According to the International Ice Cream Association, these are the top ten flavors of ice cream:

Vanilla
Chocolate
Butter Pecan
Strawberry
Neapolitan
Chocolate Chip
French Vanilla
Cookies 'n' Cream

Fudge Ripple
Praline

You'd be forgiven if you assumed, as you assume with most lists, that the top-ranked flavors did a little bit better than the others. But here's what the distribution really looked like:

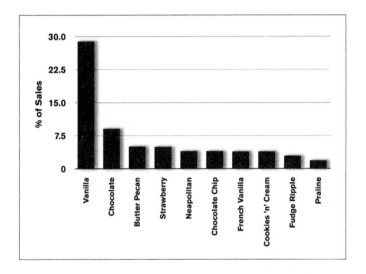

It's *always* like this (almost always, anyway). It's called Zipf's law, and it applies to résumés and college application rates and best-selling records and everything in between. Winners win big because the marketplace loves a winner.

Here's another example; these are box-office rankings from a particularly bad week at the movies in August 2006:

Invincible
Talladega Nights: The Ballad of Ricky Bobby
Little Miss Sunshine
Beerfest
World Trade Center
Accepted
Snakes on a Plane
Step Up
Idlewild
Barnyard

It's hard to feel sorry for the horrible movie *Beerfest*. After all, it came in fourth. But look at the chart of actual revenue:

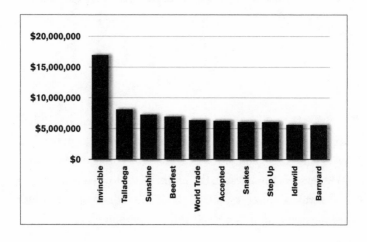

If you've read Chris Anderson's *The Long Tail*, this isn't news to you. But I don't care about the long tail right now—I want to show you the short head. The short, big, profitable head. That's the juicy share of the market that belongs to the people at the top of the list.

The Reason Number One Matters

People don't have a lot of time and don't want to take a lot of risks. If you've been diagnosed with cancer of the navel, you're not going to mess around by going to a lot of doctors. You're going to head straight for the "top guy," the person who's ranked the best in the world. Why screw around if you get only one chance?

When you visit a new town, are you the sort of person who wants to visit a typical restaurant, or do you ask the concierge for the best place?

When you're hiring someone for your team, do you ask your admin to give you the average résumé, or do you ask him to screen out all but the very best qualified people?

With limited time or opportunity to experiment, we intentionally narrow our choices to those at the top.

You're not the only person who looks for the best choice. Everyone does. As a result, the rewards for being first are enormous. It's not a linear scale. It's not a matter of getting a little more after giving a little more. It's a curve, and a steep one.

The (Real) Reason Number One Matters

The second reason there are such tremendous benefits to being number one is a little more subtle. Being at the top matters because there's room at the top for only a few. *Scarcity makes being at the top worth something.* There are hundreds of brands of bottled water, and they're all mostly the same. So we don't shop around for bottled water. There is no top for bottled water. Champagne is a different story. Dom Pérignon is at or near the top, so we pay extra for it.

Where does the scarcity come from? It comes from the hurdles that the markets and our society set up. It comes from the fact that most competitors quit long before they've created something that makes it to the top. That's the way it's supposed to be. The system depends on it.

The Best in the World?

Anyone who is going to hire you, buy from you, recommend you, vote for you, or do what you want them to do is going to wonder if you're the best choice.

Best as in: best for them, right now, based on what they believe and what they know. And *in the world* as in: their world, the world they have access to.

So if I'm looking for a freelance copy editor, I want the best copy editor in English, who's available, who can find a way to work with me at a price I can afford. That's my *best in the world.* If I want a hernia doctor, I want the doctor who is best because she's recommended by my friends or colleagues and because she fits my picture of what a great doctor is. That, and she has to be in my town and have a slot open. So *world* is a pretty flexible term.

The mass market is dying. There is no longer one best song or one best kind of coffee. Now there are a million micromarkets, but each micromarket still has a *best.* If your micromarket is "organic markets in Tulsa," then that's your world. And being the best in *that* world is the place to be.

Best is subjective. I (the consumer) get to decide, not you. *World* is selfish. It's my definition, not yours. It's the world I define, based on my convenience or my preferences. Be the best in my world and you have me, at a premium, right now.

The world is getting larger because I can now look *everywhere* when I want to find something (or someone). That means that the amount of variety is staggering, and it means I can define my world to be exactly what I have an interest in—and find my preferences anywhere on the planet.

At the same time, the world is getting smaller because the categories are getting more specialized. I can now find the best gluten-free bialys available by overnight shipping. I can find the best risk-management software for my industry, right now, online. I can find the best clothing-optional resort in North America with six clicks of a mouse. So while it's more important than ever to be the best in the world, it's also easier—*if* you pick the right thing and do it all the way. More places to win, and the stakes are higher, too.

Andy Warhol was the best in the world. So is the Sripraphai Thai restaurant in Queens. So is my editor. So are you, if you want to be. If you're not sold on being the best in the world, you probably don't need the rest of what I'm about to tell you. But if you're sold on being the best, but you've been frustrated in the route you're taking to get there, then you need to start doing some quitting.

The Infinity Problem

The problem with infinity is that there's too much of it.

And in just about every market, the number of choices is approaching infinity. Faced with infinity, people panic. Sometimes they don't buy anything. Sometimes they buy the cheapest one of whatever they're shopping for. Faced with an infinite number of choices, many people pick the market leader. Best-selling books still outsell backlist titles. Web sites highlighted on Digg still get a hundred times as much traffic as ordinary sites. Big insurance companies get clients just because they're big.

The number of job seekers is approaching infinity. So is the number of professional services firms, lawyers, manicure shops, coffee bars, and brands of soap. Better to be the best.

only talented people fret
about mediocrity.

@hugh

Is That the Best You Can Do?

Job applications in ALL CAPITAL LETTERS. Junk mail with a misspelled name. Salespeople who are eager to open an account, but never follow up. Doctors that don't bother to call to see if a new medication worked for a long-time patient. People settle. They settle for less than they are capable of. Organizations settle too. For *good enough* instead of *best in the world*.

If you're not going to put in the effort to be my best possible choice, why bother?

Is "Well, no one better showed up" a valid strategy for success? Are you hoping to become a success because you're the only one being considered?

The reason that big companies almost always fail when

they try to enter new markets is their willingness to compromise. They figure that because they are big and powerful, they can settle, do less, stop improving something before it is truly remarkable. They compromise to avoid offending other divisions or to minimize their exposure. So they fail. They fail because they don't know when to quit and when to refuse to settle.

The Biggest Mistake They Made in School

Just about everything you learned in school about life is wrong, but the wrongest thing might very well be this: Being well rounded is the secret to success.

When you came home from school with two As, a B+, and three Bs, you were doing just fine. Imagine the poor kid who had an A+ and four Cs. Boy, was he in trouble.

Fast-forward a few decades from those school days, and think about the decisions you make today—about which doctor to pick, which restaurant to visit, or which accountant to hire. How often do you look for someone who is actually quite good at the things you don't need her to do? How often do you hope that your accountant is a safe driver and a decent golfer?

In a free market, we reward the exceptional.

In school, we tell kids that once something gets too hard, move on and focus on the next thing. The low-hanging fruit is there to be taken; no sense wasting time climbing the tree.

From a test-taking book: "Skim through the questions and answer the easiest ones first, skipping ones you don't know immediately." Bad advice. Superstars can't skip the ones they don't know. In fact, the people who are the best in the world specialize at getting really good at the questions they don't know. The people who skip the hard questions are in the majority, but they are not in demand.

Many organizations make sure they've dotted all their i's—they have customer service, a receptionist, a convenient location, a brochure, and on and on—and all of it is mediocre. More often than not, prospects choose someone else—their competition. Those competitors can't perform in some areas, but they're exceptional in the ones that matter.

The Magic of Thinking Quit

Twenty years ago, I read a book that changed my life. It was called *The Magic of Thinking Big*. I actually don't remember anything about the book at all. What I do remember is that in one quick moment, it changed the way I thought about success.

My hope is that the next page or two might do the same for you. I want to change the way you think about success (and quitting).

Most people will tell you that you need to persevere—to try harder, put in more hours, get more training, and work hard. "Don't quit!" they implore. But if all you need to do to succeed is not quit, then why do organizations less motivated than yours succeed? Why do individuals less talented than you win?

It involves understanding the architecture of quitting, and, believe it or not, it means quitting a lot more than you do now.

Strategic quitting is the secret of successful organizations. Reactive quitting and serial quitting are the bane of those that strive (and fail) to get what they want. And most people do just that. They quit when it's painful and stick when they can't be bothered to quit.

There are two curves that define almost any type of situation facing you as you try to accomplish something. (A couple of minor curves cover the rest.) Understanding the different types of situations that lead you to quit—or that should cause you to quit—is the first step toward getting what you want.

CURVE 1: THE DIP

Almost everything in life worth doing is controlled by the Dip.

It looks like this:

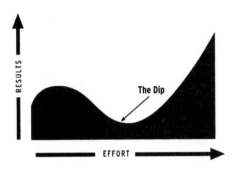

At the beginning, when you first start something, it's fun. You could be taking up golf or acupuncture or piloting a plane or doing chemistry—doesn't matter; it's interesting, and you get plenty of good feedback from the people around you.

Over the next few days and weeks, the rapid learning you experience keeps you going. Whatever your new thing is, it's easy to stay engaged in it.

And then the Dip happens.

The Dip is the long slog between starting and mastery. A long slog that's actually a shortcut, because it gets you where you want to go faster than any other path.

The Dip is the combination of bureaucracy and busywork you must deal with in order to get certified in scuba diving.

The Dip is the difference between the easy "beginner"

technique and the more useful "expert" approach in skiing or fashion design.

The Dip is the long stretch between beginner's luck and real accomplishment.

The Dip is the set of artificial screens set up to keep people like you out.

If you took organic chemistry in college, you've experienced the Dip. Academia doesn't want too many unmotivated people to attempt medical school, so they set up a screen. Organic chemistry is the killer class, the screen that separates the doctors from the psychologists. If you can't handle organic chemistry, well, then, you can't go to med school.

At the beginning, when you announce that you're premed, you get all sorts of positive feedback and support. Your grandmother can't believe her good fortune! But soon, the incredible grind of organic chemistry kicks in, and you realize you're doomed.

At trade shows, you see dozens of companies trying to break into an industry. They've invested time and money to build a product, to create a marketing organization and rent booth space—all in an attempt to break into a lucrative market. A year later, most of them don't return. They're gone, unable to get through the Dip.

The same thing happens to people who dream of the untold riches and power that accrue to the CEO of a Fortune 500 company. Private jets, fancy country clubs, unchecked decision-making power. Who wouldn't want to live like modern-day royalty? Of course, if you look at the résumé of a typical CEO, you'll see that he endured a twenty-five-year Dip before landing the job. For a quarter of a century, he needed to suck it up, keep his head down, and do what he was told. He needed to hit his numbers, work longer hours than everyone else, and kiss up to his boss of the moment. Day in and day out, year after year.

It's easy to be a CEO. What's hard is getting there. There's a huge Dip along the way. If it was easy, there'd be too many people vying for the job and the CEOs couldn't get paid as much, could they? Scarcity, as we've seen, is the secret to value. If there wasn't a Dip, there'd be no scarcity.

IMPORTANT NOTE: Successful people don't just ride out the Dip. They don't just buckle down and survive it. No, they lean into the Dip. They push harder, changing the rules as they go. Just because you know you're in the Dip doesn't mean you have to live happily with it. Dips don't last quite as long when you whittle at them.

CURVE 2: THE CUL-DE-SAC

The Cul-de-Sac (French for "dead end") is so simple it doesn't even need a chart. It's a situation where you work and you work and you work and nothing much changes. It doesn't get a lot better, it doesn't get a lot worse. It just is.

That's why they call those jobs dead-end jobs.

There's not a lot to say about the Cul-de-Sac except to realize that it exists and to embrace the fact that when you find one, you need to get off it, fast. That's because a dead end is keeping you from doing something else. The opportunity cost of investing your life in something that's not going to get better is just too high.

That's it. Two big curves (a bonus, the Cliff, follows). Stick with the Dips that are likely to pan out, and quit the Cul-de-Sacs to focus your resources. That's it.

CURVE 3: THE CLIFF (RARE BUT SCARY)

Cigarettes, it turns out, were redesigned by scientists to be particularly addictive. If you were going to draw a chart of the pleasure of smoking over time, it would look like this:

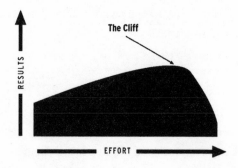

Except for that nasty drop-off at the end (otherwise known as emphysema), smoking is a marketer's dream come true. Because smoking is designed to be almost impossible to quit, the longer you do it, the better it feels to continue smoking. The pain of quitting just gets bigger and bigger over time. I call this curve a Cliff—it's a situation where you can't quit until you fall off, and the whole thing falls apart.

It's no wonder that people have trouble stopping.

The thing is, a profession in selling isn't like smoking cigarettes. Neither is making it as a singer or building a long-term relationship with someone you care about. Most of the time, the other two curves are in force. The Dip and the Cul-de-Sac aren't linear. They don't spoon feed you with little bits of improvement every day. And they're just waiting to trip you up.

If It Is Worth Doing, There's Probably a Dip

Tennis has a Dip. The difference between a mediocre club player and a regional champion isn't inborn talent—it's the ability to push through the moments where it's just easier to quit. Politics has a Dip as well—it's way more fun to win an election than to lose one, and the entire process is built around many people starting while most people quit.

The Dip creates scarcity; scarcity creates value.

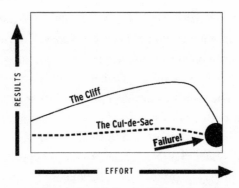

The Cul-de-Sac is boring, the Cliff is exciting
(for a while), but neither gets you through the Dip
and both lead to failure

The Cul-de-Sac and the Cliff Are the Curves That Lead to Failure

If you find yourself facing either of these two curves, you need to quit. Not soon, but right now. The biggest obstacle to success in life, as far as I can tell, is our inability to quit these curves soon enough.

It's easy to complain that the advice in this little book is brain-dead obvious. I mean, who doesn't already know that the secret to success is to be successful, that providing a great product or service is the right thing to do, and that you shouldn't quit in the face of adversity?

You don't. That's the bad news. The good news is that your boss and your competitors don't know either.

I mean, you *know* it, but my guess is that you're not doing anything about it. When it comes right down to it, right down to the hard decisions, are you quitting any project that isn't a Dip? Or is it just easier not to rock the boat, to hang in there, to avoid the short-term hassle of changing paths? What's the point of sticking it out if you're not going to get the benefits of being the best in the world? Are you over-investing (really significantly overinvesting) time and money so that you have a much greater chance of dominating a market? And if you don't have enough time and money, do you have the guts to pick a different, smaller market to conquer?

Once you're doing those things, *then* you get it.

The Dip Is Where Success Happens

If you haven't already realized it, the Dip is the secret to your success. The people who set out to make it through the Dip—the people who invest the time and the energy and the effort to power through the Dip—those are the ones who become the best in the world. They are breaking the system because, instead of moving on to the next thing, instead of doing slightly above average and settling for what they've got, they embrace the challenge. For whatever reason, they refuse to abandon the quest and they push through the Dip all the way to the next level.

Snowboarding is a hip sport. It's fast, exciting, and reasonably priced; and it makes you look very cool. So why are there so few snowboarders? Because learning the basic skills constitutes a painful Dip. It takes a few days to get the hang of it, and, during those few days, you'll get pretty banged up. It's easier to quit than it is to keep going.

The *brave* thing to do is to tough it out and end up on the other side—getting all the benefits that come from scarcity. The *mature* thing is not even to bother starting to snowboard because you're probably not going to make it through the Dip. And the *stupid* thing to do is to start, give it your best shot, waste a lot of time and money, and quit right in the middle of the Dip.

A few people will choose to do the brave thing and end up the best in the world. Informed people will probably choose to do the mature thing and save their resources for a project they're truly passionate about. Both are fine choices. It's the last choice, the common choice, the choice to give it a shot and then quit that you must avoid if you want to succeed.

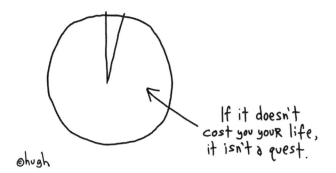

If it doesn't cost you your life, it isn't a quest.

©hugh

What Butch Knew

When Butch Cassidy and the Sundance Kid were being chased across the Badlands by Charlie Siringo and agents from Pinkerton's, Butch kept heading for the hills, for tougher and tougher terrain. Why? Because he knew that in open country, he and Sundance would never have a shot at escape. Only if they got through the impassable hills ahead would there be a chance that the Pinkerton's guys would quit. The harder it got, the better it was for Butch.

But the Pinkerton's posse persisted. It wasn't until Butch and Sundance faced certain death that they escaped. Hey, it worked in the movie. Your marketplace is competitive, filled with people overcoming challenges every day. It's the incredibly difficult challenges (the Dips) that give you the opportunity to pull ahead.

In a competitive world, adversity is your ally. The harder it gets, the better chance you have of insulating yourself from the competition. If that adversity also causes you to quit, though, it's all for nothing.

What Jack Knew

When Jack Welch remade GE, the most fabled decision he made was this: If we can't be #1 or #2 in an industry, we must get out.

Why sell a billion-dollar division that's making a profit quite happily while ranking #4 in market share? Easy. Because it distracts management attention. It sucks resources and capital and focus and energy. And most of all, it teaches people in the organization that it's okay not to be the best in the world.

Jack quit the dead ends. By doing so, he freed resources to get his other businesses through the Dip.

The Thing About the Wind

I can tell you that windsurfing is very easy—except for the wind.

The wind makes it tricky, of course. It's not particularly

difficult to find and rent great equipment, and the techniques are fairly straightforward. What messes the whole plan up is the fact that the wind is unpredictable. It'll change exactly when you don't want it to.

The same thing is true about customer service (it would be a lot easier if it weren't for the customers). In fact, every single function of an organization has a wind problem.

Accounting would be easy if every incoming report were accurate and on time. Sales would be easy if it weren't for the prospects not buying from you all the time. Marketing would be easy if every prospect and customer thought the way you do.

Here's the good news: The fact that it's difficult and unpredictable works to your advantage. Because if it were any other way, there'd be no profit in it. The reason people bother to go windsurfing is that the challenge makes it interesting. The driving force that gets people to pay a specialist is that their disease is unpredictable or hard to diagnose. The reason we're here is to solve the hard problems.

The next time you're tempted to vilify a particularly obnoxious customer or agency or search engine, realize that this failed interaction is the best thing that's happened to you all day long. Without it, you'd be easily replaceable. The Dip is your very best friend.

The Reason We're Here

If I could offer just one piece of inspiration, it's this: The Dip is the reason you're here. Whether you're lifting weights or negotiating a sale or applying for a job or lunging for a tennis ball, you've made a huge investment. You've invested time and money and effort to get to this moment. You've acquired the equipment and the education and the reputation . . . all so you can confront this Dip, right now.

The Dip is the reason you're here.

It's not enough to survive your way through this Dip. You get what you deserve when you embrace the Dip and treat it like the opportunity that it really is.

The Lie of Diversification–
What Woodpeckers Know

When faced with the Dip, many individuals and organizations diversify. If you can't get to the next level, the thinking goes, invest your energy in learning to do something else. This leads to record labels with thousands of artists instead of focused promotion for just a few. It leads to job seekers who can demonstrate competency at a dozen tasks instead of mastery of just one.

Hardworking, motivated people find diversification a

natural outlet for their energy and drive. Diversification feels like the right thing to do. Enter a new market, apply for a job in a new area, start a new sport. Who knows? This might just be the one.

And yet the real success goes to those who obsess. The focus that leads you through the Dip to the other side is rewarded by a marketplace in search of the best in the world.

A woodpecker can tap twenty times on a thousand trees and get nowhere, but stay busy. Or he can tap twenty-thousand times on one tree and get dinner.

Before you enter a new market, consider what would happen if you managed to get through the Dip and win in the market you're already in.

Most People Are Afraid to Quit

It's easier to be mediocre than it is to confront reality and quit.

Quitting is difficult. Quitting requires you to acknowledge that you're never going to be #1 in the world. At least not at this. So it's easier just to put it off, not admit it, settle for mediocre.

What a waste.

You Should Be Angry Now . . .

I know that I am. I'm angry at all the worthwhile organizations that stick with a Cul-de-Sac instead of leaving it and investing their resources where they belong. I'm angry at all the people who have wasted time and money trying to get through a Dip that they should have realized was too big and too deep to get through with the resources they had available. Mostly I'm angry that it took me this long to be able to describe how simple the solution is.

How Arnold Beat the Dip

The essential thing to know about the Dip is that it's there. Knowing that you're facing a Dip is the first step in getting through it.

Every time *Men's Health* puts a picture of a guy with washboard abs on their cover, newsstand sales go up. Why? Well, if everyone had washboard abs, it's unlikely that men would buy a magazine that teaches them how to get that physique.

The very scarcity of this attribute makes it attractive.

Weight training is a fascinating science. Basically, you do a minute or two of work for no reason other than to tire out your muscle so that the last few seconds of work will cause that muscle to grow.

Like most people, all day long, every day, you use your muscles. But they don't grow. You don't look like Mr. Universe because you quit using your muscles before you reach the moment where the stress causes them to start growing. It's the natural thing to do, because an exhausted muscle feels unsafe—and it hurts.

People who train successfully pay their dues for the first minute or two and then get all the benefits at the very end. Unsuccessful trainers pay exactly the same dues but stop a few seconds too early.

It's human nature to quit when it hurts. But it's that reflex that creates scarcity.

The challenge is simple: Quitting when you hit the Dip is a bad idea. If the journey you started was worth doing, then quitting when you hit the Dip just wastes the time you've already invested. Quit in the Dip often enough and you'll find yourself becoming a serial quitter, starting many things but accomplishing little.

Simple: If you can't make it through the Dip, don't start.

If you can embrace that simple rule, you'll be a lot choosier about which journeys you start.

Superstar Thinking

Superstars get what they want because they have unique skills. Superstars command far more than their fair share of income, respect, and opportunity because there are very few other choices for a customer or an employer seeking the extraordinary.

A superstar real estate agent gets five or ten times the number of listings as an ordinary one. A superstar lawyer has all the work she can handle, regardless of her specialty. A superstar musician commands a thousand times the income per performance as an average musician. A superstar is the best in the world at what she does.

If you want to be a superstar, then you need to find a field with a steep Dip—a barrier between those who try and those who succeed. And you've got to get through that Dip to the other side. This isn't for everyone. If it were, there'd be no superstars. If you choose this path, it's because you realize that there's a Dip, and you believe you can get through it.

The Dip is actually your greatest ally because it makes the project worthwhile (and keeps others from competing with you).

But wait, that's not enough. Not only do you need to find a Dip that you can conquer but you also need to quit all the Cul-de-Sacs that you're currently idling your way through. You must quit the projects and investments and endeavors that don't offer you the same opportunity. It's difficult, but it's vitally important.

Being better than 98 percent of the competition used to be fine. In the world of Google, though, it's useless. It's useless because all of your competition is just a click away, whatever it is you do. The only position you can count on now is best in the world.

Seven Reasons You Might Fail to Become the Best in the World

You run out of time (and quit).

You run out of money (and quit).

You get scared (and quit).

You're not serious about it (and quit).

You lose interest or enthusiasm or settle for being mediocre (and quit).

You focus on the short term instead of the long (and quit when the short term gets too hard).

You pick the wrong thing at which to be the best in the world (because you don't have the talent).

By "you" I mean your team, your company, or just plain you, the job seeker, the employee, or the entrepreneur. The important thing to remember about these seven things is that you can plan for them. You can know *before you start* whether or not you have the resources and the will to get to the end. Most of the time, if you fail to become the best in the world, it's either because you planned wrong or because you gave up before you reached your goal.

Is it possible that you're just not good enough? That you (or your team) just don't have enough talent to be the best in the world? Sure it's possible. In fact, if your chosen area is the cello, or speed skating, then I might even say it's probable. But in just about every relevant area I can think of, no, it's not likely. You are good enough. The question is, will you take the shortcut you need to get really good at this?

Why Is the Curve with a Dip so Prevalent?

One of the underpinnings of the Dip is the pyramid. A pyramid scheme is a scam in which the people at the bottom support the guy at the top. But it's not always a scam. In fact, it happens a lot more than you realize.

For example, lots of people sign up for a health-club membership (having a lot of members lets the club keep rates reasonable), but the club itself is small because very few people actually come frequently after they join. That's built into the system. If everyone who joined came, you'd never be able to find an empty bike or to afford a membership.

Netflix gives you an unlimited number of DVD rentals a month, postage paid, for $10. How can this be? If you watched a movie the day it came in and sent it right back, you'd get to see at least six movies for $10. Of course, the key is that for every person who sees six, there are plenty of people who lose interest and see one movie, or even no movies, a month. These people subsidize the committed members. Sure, Netflix wants you to see a lot of movies—that makes you a loyal customer. But the economics of the entire business would fall apart if it weren't for the uncommitted users who just dabble.

For a long time, airlines oversold their flights because they knew they would profit from the no-shows.

Politicians fully expect that the lazy and ill-informed won't bother to vote. These citizens pay taxes, which support the political life of the few who don't quit the system.

And, of course, the entire college-football money machine is based on a pyramid scheme of players who aspire to the NFL but will never make it.

Whatever you do for a living, or for fun, it's probably somehow based on a system that's based on quitting. *Quitting creates scarcity; scarcity creates value.*

In *The Wizard of Oz*, there's an indelible image of the man behind the curtain, laughing at Dorothy and her friends as he gives them incredibly difficult, almost impossible tasks to accomplish. While he lives the easy life in Oz, he supports himself by sending his acolytes off on impossible missions.

It's no wonder we quit. The system wants us to.

Eight Dip Curves

Here are a bunch of systems that are dependent on Dips. These Dips are in the places where organizations and individuals are most likely to give up. If you see these Dips coming, you're more likely to make a choice. You can choose (in advance) to do whatever you need to do in order to get through the Dip, knowing it's going to be difficult; or you can give up before you get there. Quitting *in* the Dip, though, isn't worth the journey.

MANUFACTURING DIP—It's easy and fun to start building something in your garage. It's difficult and expensive to buy an injection mold, design an integrated circuit, or ramp up for large-scale production. The time and effort and cost of ramping up your operation create the Dip. The Dip keeps the supply of stuff down and insulates those brave enough to invest in scaling up their production. Those struggling artists at the local craft fair are struggling because they don't have the guts or the wherewithal to take their work to the next level.

SALES DIP—Most ideas get their start when one person— you—starts selling it. Selling the idea to stores or to businesses or to consumers or even to voters. But the Dip hits when you need to upgrade to a professional sales force and scale it up. In almost every field, the competitor that's first with a big, aggressive sales force has a huge advantage.

EDUCATION DIP—A career gets started as soon as you leave school. But the Dip often hits when it's time to go learn something new, to reinvent or rebuild your skills. A doctor who sacrifices a year of her life for a specialty reaps the rewards for decades afterward.

RISK DIP—Bootstrappers learn the hard way that at some point they can't pay for it all themselves, especially out of current income. It takes a risk to rent a bigger space or invest in new techniques. Successful entrepreneurs understand the difference between investing to get through the Dip (a smart move) or investing in something that's actually a risky crapshoot.

RELATIONSHIP DIP—There are people and organizations that can help you later but only if you invest the time and effort to work with them now, even though now is not necessarily the easy time for you to do it. That kid who started in the mail room—who was always eager to do an errand for you or stay late to help out—she's now the CEO. The relationships she built when it was difficult to do so paid off later. Those shortsighted people who are always eager for a favor or a break never manage to get through the relationship Dip, because they didn't invest in relationships back when it was difficult (but not urgent).

CONCEPTUAL DIP—You got this far operating under one set of assumptions. Abandoning those assumptions and embracing a new, bigger set may be exactly what you need to do to get to the next level. The heroes who have reinvented institutions and industries (everyone from Martin Luther King, Jr., to Richard Branson, from Zelma Watson George to Jacqueline Novogratz) all did it in exactly the same way—by working through a conceptual Dip all the way to the other side.

EGO DIP—When it's all about you, it's easier. Giving up control and leaning into the organization gives you leverage. Most people can't do this; they can't give up control or the spotlight. They get stuck in that Dip.

DISTRIBUTION DIP—Some retailers (local strip malls, the Web) make it easy for your product to get distribution, while others (Target) require an investment from your organization that may just pay off. Getting your product into Wal-Mart is far more likely to lead to huge sales than is putting it on the Web. Why? Scarcity. Everyone is on the Web, but getting into Wal-Mart is hard.

Seeing the Curve in Advance

As you'll see in the space-shuttle analysis that follows, it's pretty easy to determine whether something is a Cul-de-Sac or a Dip. The hard part is finding the guts to do something about it. Optimistic entrepreneurs and employees who blithely wander into a serious business, totally out-gunned and unprepared to work their way through the Dip ahead, are in danger of building a space shuttle.

There's nothing wrong with optimism. The pain (and the waste) comes when the optimists have to make hard choices when they get stuck in the Dip.

Time to Cancel the Space Shuttle

The space shuttle is a Cul-de-Sac, not a Dip. When pundits argue in favor of the shuttle, they don't say, "We should keep doing this because it's going to get safer/cheaper/more pro-ductive over time." The only reason the shuttle still exists is that no one has the guts to cancel it. There's no reason to keep investing in something that is not going to get better.

In fact, if we canceled the shuttle, we'd create an urgent need for a replacement. The lack of a way to get to space would force us to invent a new, better, cheaper alternative.

So why don't we cancel it? Why not quit? Same reason as always. Because day to day, it's easier to stick with something that we're used to, that doesn't make too many waves, that doesn't hurt.

As the Declaration of Independence warns us, "all experi-ence hath shewn that mankind are more disposed to suffer,

while evils are sufferable, than to right themselves by abol-
ishing the forms to which they are accustomed."

Do you have the guts to quit when facing a Cul-de-Sac?

The Valley of Death

That's the goal of any competitor: to create a Dip so long
and so deep that the nascent competition can't catch up.

Microsoft does it. They've built so many relationships
and established so many standards that it's essentially incon-
ceivable that someone will challenge Word or Excel—at least
until the platform changes. Intuit made it through the Dip,
though, and now their Quicken accounting software is just as
secure as Word is as a word processor. Make it through the
competition's barriers and you get to be king for a while.

"But wait!" you say. "Isn't Google going hard after Microsoft by creating Web-based versions of spreadsheets and
word processors?" Yes. But even mighty Google knows that
they can't do that without changing the platform (from the
PC to the Web). Microsoft has constructed a Dip so deep
and so expensive that it's impossible to cross. But now, with a
new platform, Google has a much easier path to follow.

Apple's done the same thing with iTunes and the iPod.
First, they took advantage of a new platform to destroy the
Tower Records of the world. Then, instead of resting on

their lead, Apple built all sorts of systems and benefits that make it extremely difficult for someone to persevere long enough to come out ahead at the other end.

Professions do it as well. Lawyers, for example, have continually increased how difficult it is to pass the bar exam, lengthening the Dip and making life better on the other side for everyone who is already a lawyer.

The Big Opportunity

If you can get through the Dip, if you can keep going when the system is expecting you to stop, you will achieve extraordinary results. People who make it through the Dip are scarce indeed, so they generate more value.

When you're the best in the world, you share the benefits (the income, the attention, the privileges, the respect) with just a handful of people or organizations or brands. That male magazine model with the great abs gets work precisely because so many people have quit in their quest to get what he's got.

You know this already. You're not stupid, and you've noticed all your life that the big benefits accrue to those who don't quit. And it hasn't made a difference so far, so why should you listen to me now?

Simple. It's about the story you tell yourself. You grew up believing that quitting is a moral failing. Quitting feels like a go-down moment, a moment where you look yourself in the eye and blink. *Of course* you are trying your best. But you just can't do it. It's that whole Vince Lombardi thing. If you were just a better person, you wouldn't quit.

I'd rather have you focus on quitting (or not quitting) as a *go-up* opportunity. It's not about avoiding the humiliation of failure. Even more important, you can realize that quitting the stuff you don't care about or the stuff you're mediocre at or better yet quitting the Cul-de-Sacs frees up your resources to obsess about the Dips that matter.

If you're going to quit, quit before you start. Reject the system. Don't play the game if you realize you can't be the best in the world.

Average Is for Losers

Quitting at the right time is difficult. Most of us don't have the guts to quit. Worse, when faced with the Dip, sometimes we don't quit. Instead, we get mediocre.

The most common response to the Dip is to play it safe. To do ordinary work, blameless work, work that's beyond reproach. When faced with the Dip, most people suck it up and try to average their way to success.

Which is precisely why so few people end up as the best in the world.

To be a superstar, you must do something exceptional.

But what if
I fail?

We all get
to laugh
at you.

@hugh

Not just *survive* the Dip, but use the Dip as an opportunity to create something so extraordinary that people can't help but talk about it, recommend it, and, yes, choose it.

The next time you catch yourself being average when you feel like quitting, realize that you have only two good choices: Quit or be exceptional. Average is for losers.

Am I being too harsh? Isn't your time and your effort and your career and your reputation too valuable to squander on just being average? Average feels safe, but it's not. It's invisible. It's the last choice—the path of least resistance. The temptation to be average is just another kind of quitting . . . the kind to be avoided. You deserve better than average.

Serial Quitters Spend a Lot of Time in Line

Observing the supermarket over the years, I've determined that there are three common checkout strategies. My local supermarket may be like yours—it usually has four or five checkouts open. If you watch carefully, you'll see people adopting one of three strategies:

The first is to pick the shortest line and get in it. Stick with it, no matter what.

The second is to pick the shortest line and switch lines once (at a maximum) if something holds up your line—like the clueless person with a check but no check-cashing card. But that's it, just one switch.

The third is to pick the shortest line and keep scanning the other lines. Switch lines if a shorter one appears. Continue this process until you leave the store.

The problem with the third strategy is obvious. Every time you switch lines, you're starting over. In your search for a quick fix, you almost certainly waste time and you definitely waste energy jumping back and forth.

There are queues everywhere. Do you know an entrepreneur-wannabe who is on his sixth or twelfth new project? He jumps from one to another, and every time he hits an obstacle, he switches to a new, easier, better opportunity. And while he's a seeker, he's never going to get anywhere.

He never gets anywhere because he's always switching lines, never able to really run for it. While starting up is thrilling, it's not until you get through the Dip that your efforts pay off. Countless entrepreneurs have perfected the starting part, but give up long before they finish paying their dues. The sad news is that when you start over, you get very little credit for how long you stood in line with your last great venture.

This malady doesn't afflict just entrepreneurs. Advertisers who are always jumping from one agency to another, or one medium to another, end up wasting a fortune. If it takes ten impressions to make an impact, and you've delivered eight, that switch is going to cost you a lot of time and money.

Salespeople Who Quit

A well-reported study (probably apocryphal) found that the typical salesperson gives up after the fifth contact with a prospect. After five times, the salesperson figures she's wasting her time and the prospect's, quits, and moves on.

Of course, the study reports that 80 percent of these customers buy on the seventh attempt to close the sale. If only the salesperson had stuck it out!

Is it true that people need to be closed constantly, that seven is a magic number, and that the key to selling is to be aggressive? I don't think so. I don't think the best salespeople are the ones who are always in your face, always asking for the order, always pushing.

I think the lesson of the story is this: Selling is about a transference of emotion, not a presentation of facts. If it were just a presentation of facts, then a PDF flyer or a Web site would be sufficient to make the phone ring.

Prospects (that's you if you've ever been sold something) are experts at sensing what's on the salesperson's mind. People have honed their salesperson radar—we're really good at detecting sincerity (or the lack of it). If a salesperson's attitude is "Hey, if this person doesn't buy, there's someone right down the street I can call on," what's projected is "Hey, I'm not that serious about you having this product." On the other hand, if a salesperson is there for the long run, committed to making a sale because it benefits the other person, that signal is sent loud and clear.

Please understand this: If you're not able to get through the Dip in an exceptional way, you *must* quit. And quit right now. Because if your order book is 80 percent filled with prospects where you just sort of show up, you're not only wasting your time, you're also stealing your energy from the 20 percent of the calls where you have a chance to create a breakthrough.

Once again, getting through the Dip is a valid strategy. It isn't a good strategy because successful salespeople are annoying—no, sticking through the Dip is a great strategy because it changes the entire dynamic of the salesperson's day. It is not a moral choice. It's a strategic one. "I'm getting through this Dip with you because it's important to both of us" is the very best signal to send.

Facing the Dip

You may be sure that your product is the best in the world, but no one outside a tiny group cares at all. You're busy pushing your new idea wherever it can go. Meanwhile, most consumers could care less about your idea or those fancy high-heeled shoes or some cutting-edge type of glue. Instead, they wait. They wait for something to be standardized, tested, inexpensive, and ready for prime time.

Hence the Dip of market acceptance. The marketers who get rewarded are the ones who don't quit. They hunker down through the Dip and galvanize and insulate and perfect their product while others keep looking for yet another quick hit.

So while one publisher runs from author to author looking for an instant best seller, another nurtures Dr. Seuss or Stephen King as he slowly builds an audience. While one nonprofit runs from grant maker to grant maker seeking funds for this project or that one, a successful nonprofit sticks with a consistent theme, showing up, paying its dues, focusing on just a few foundations until the money comes through.

Gorilla Glue made it through the Dip. So did Jimmy Choo and the Swatch. Not overnight, but bit by bit, until they reached a critical mass.

Job seekers face the Dip because human resources departments support it. HR doesn't show up at your door and offer you a job. They set hurdles (like submitting a résumé or wearing a suit or flying to Cleveland) as a way of screening out the folks who aren't actually serious about a job.

We're seduced by the tales of actresses being discovered at the local drugstore, or a classmate who got a fantastic job just by showing up at the college placement office. We see an author hit the big time after just one appearance on *Oprah* or a rock band getting signed after submitting a demo—it all seems easy and exciting.

It's easy to be seduced by the new money and the rush to the fresh. The problem is that this leads to both an addiction and a very short attention span. If it doesn't work today, the thinking goes, why should I wait around until tomorrow? The problem is that only a tiny portion of the audience is looking for the brand-new thing. Most people are waiting for the tested, the authenticated, and the proven.

Very quietly, the Microsofts of the world hang in, going from version 1 to version 2, knowing that by version 3, the

world will be a different (and better) place for them. Microsoft failed twice with Windows, four times with Word, three times with Excel. The entire company is based on the idea of slogging through the Dip, relentlessly changing tactics but never quitting the big idea.

What Business Are You In?

Yes, you should (you must) quit a product or a feature or a design—you need to do it regularly if you're going to grow and have the resources to invest in the right businesses. But no, you mustn't quit a market or a strategy or a niche. The businesses we think of as overnight successes weren't. We just didn't notice them until they were well baked.

Procter & Gamble has killed hundreds of products. Starbucks killed their music-CD–burning stations. Social Security reform has been dropped a dozen times. Don't fall in love with a tactic and defend it forever. Instead, decide once and for all whether you're in a market or not. And if you are, get through that Dip.

The market wants to see you persist. It demands a signal from you that you're serious, powerful, accepted, and safe. The bulk of the market, any market, is made up of those folks in the middle of the bell curve, the ones who want to buy something proven and valued.

Following a product all the way through the Dip works because you're reaching an ever larger part of the market. If your product isn't working, if your service isn't catching on, if you're not even appealing to the crazy geeks who like the new stuff, you mustn't persist with a tactic just because you feel stuck with it. Your strategy—to be a trusted source in your chosen market—can survive even if your product is canceled.

The Opposite of Quitting Isn't "Waiting Around"

No, the opposite of quitting is *rededication*. The opposite of quitting is *an invigorated new strategy designed to break the problem apart.*

It's a mistake to view the Dip as static, to imagine that you are merely a passive passenger on a slow-moving boat ride, sitting there as you move through the doldrums of the Dip.

The Dip is flexible. It responds to the effort you put into it. In fact, it's quite likely (in almost every case) that aggressive action on your part can make the Dip a lot worse. Or a lot better. Let's try for better.

When the pain gets so bad that you're ready to quit, you've set yourself up as someone with nothing to lose. And someone with nothing to lose has quite a bit of power. You can go for broke. Challenge authority. Attempt unattempted alternatives. Lean into a problem; lean so far that you might just lean right through it.

David found himself stuck in a dead-end job at the end of a long career at one company, and he was ready to quit. His boss was a disaster, the work wasn't adding any value to his résumé or his day, and he was unhappy. David went for broke. He had a meeting with his boss and his boss's boss (quite a no-no) and calmly explained his problem. He said that he figured he'd end up quitting, but he liked the company so much he wanted to propose an alternative. So he did.

He walked out with a major promotion, a brand-new challenge, and a new boss.

If he had covered his downside, worried about the short term, and not been prepared to quit that very day, it never would have happened. He wasn't bluffing. He really was ready either to quit or to lean into this new job, to rededicate himself to the company and make something happen.

Quitting in the Dip Is Usually a Short-term Decision—and a Bad One

When people quit, they are often focused on the short-term benefits. In other words, "If it hurts; stop!"

When Joe Biden quit the race for president in 1988, it was over an issue that seems incredibly trivial today—he didn't give proper attribution to a quote in a speech. But at that moment, the pain was overwhelming, and Biden and his advisers couldn't see a way from here to there. So they quit. Eighteen years later, Biden is talking about running again. What a shame. If he had realized in 1988 that he was in a situation where he had nothing to lose, he could have radically changed the conversation around the campaign. If he had changed the Dip, by forcing his way through it, he'd have had a chance to leave his opponents behind.

When a kid drops out of football or karate, it's not because she's carefully considered the long-term consequences of her action. She does it because her coach keeps yelling at her, and it's not fun. It's better to stop.

Short-term pain has more impact on most people than long-term benefits do, which is why it's so important for you to amplify the long-term benefits of not quitting. You need to remind yourself of life at the other end of the Dip because it's easier to overcome the pain of yet another unsuccessful cold call if the reality of a successful sales career is more concrete.

It's easier to stick out a lousy class in college if you can picture graduation day. Even more vivid is the power of keeping score. If you can track your Alexa rank online or your class rank or your market share or your spot in the sales-team pecking order, working your way up to number one is daily feedback that helps you deal with the short-term hassles.

No One Quits the Boston Marathon at Mile 25

It's not hard to imagine what the drop-out curve for the marathon looks like. Probably something like this:

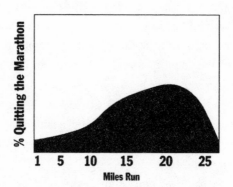

The Dip is not just before the finish line. It is at mile 20. Once you can see the crowd at the end, finishing is easier.

Who, after all, is going to drop out when the finish line is in sight?

Persistent people are able to visualize the idea of light at the end of the tunnel when others can't see it. At the same time, the smartest people are realistic about not imagining light when there isn't any.

If you work at a big city newspaper, you can see that there's no light at the end of that career-choice tunnel. Circulation is dropping, and it's going to drop ever faster. Most papers have little chance of replacing their traditional business with an online alternative. As a result, every day at most papers is going to be just a little bit worse than the day before. Every day you stay is a bad strategic decision for your career because every day you get better at something that isn't that useful—and you are another day behind others who are learning something more useful. The only reason to stay is the short-term pain associated with quitting. Winners understand that taking that pain now prevents a lot more pain later.

The same applies to the strategic management of organizations. The decision to quit or not is a simple evaluation: Is the pain of the Dip worth the benefit of the light at the end of the tunnel?

If You're Not Going to Get to #1, You Might as Well Quit Now.

QUIT!

It's okay to quit, sometimes.

In fact, it's okay to quit often.

You should quit if you're on a dead-end path. You should quit if you're facing a Cliff. You should quit if the project you're working on has a Dip that isn't worth the reward at the end. Quitting the projects that don't go anywhere is essential if you want to stick out the right ones. You don't have the time or the passion or the resources to be the best in the world at both.

Quitting a Tactic vs. Quitting a Strategy

Yes, I know it's heretical, but I'm advocating quitting. Quitting often, in fact.

Not giving up and abandoning your long-term strategy (wherever you might be using that strategy—a career, an income, a relationship, a sale) but quitting the tactics that aren't working.

Getting off a Cul-de-Sac is not a moral failing. It's just smart. Seeing a Cliff coming far in advance isn't a sign of weakness. Instead, it represents real insight and bravery. It frees up your energy for the Dip.

That Noise Inside Your Head

Right at this moment, my clairvoyance tells me you're having a conversation that involves a lot of rationalization. You're explaining to yourself why those Cul-de-Sacs you're in aren't really dead ends (they are). You're busy defending the mediocre work your organization does because it's the best you can do under the circumstances (it's not). You don't want to quit. It's not fun. It's not easy. So you haven't. But you should. You must!

Or, you could just settle for being average.

Quitting as an Intelligent Strategy

Doug just got another promotion. He works for a software company in Indiana, and, over the last fourteen years, he's had a wide range of jobs. For the first seven or eight years,

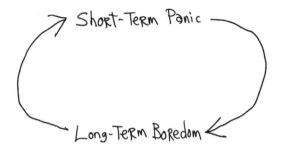

@hugh

Doug was in business development and sales. He handled the Microsoft account for a while, flying to Redmond, Washington, every six weeks or so. It was hard on his family, but he's really focused—and really good.

Two years ago, Doug got a huge promotion. He was put in charge of his entire division—150 people, the second-biggest group in the company. Doug attacked the job with relish. In addition to spending even more time on the road, he did a great job of handling internal management issues.

A month ago, for a variety of good reasons, Doug got a sideways promotion. Same level, but a new team of analysts report to him. Now he's in charge of strategic alliances. He's well respected, he's done just about every job, and he makes a lot of money.

Imagine the conversation you could have with him. "You've been there a long time, my friend."

Doug won't buy it: "Yes, I've been here fourteen years, but I've had seven jobs. When I got here, we were a start-up, but now we're a division of Cisco. I've got new challenges, and the commute is great . . ."

Go on, interrupt him.

Doug needs to leave for a very simple reason. He's been branded. Everyone at the company has an expectation of who Doug is and what he can do. Working your way up from the mail room sounds sexy; but, in fact, it's entirely unlikely. Doug has hit a plateau. He's not going to be challenged, pushed, or promoted to president. Doug, regardless of what he could actually accomplish, has stopped evolving—at least in the eyes of the people who matter.

If he leaves and joins another company, he gets to reinvent himself. No one in the new company will remember young Doug from ten years ago. No, they'll treat Doug as the new Doug, the Doug with an endless upside and little past.

Our parents and grandparents believed you should stay at a job for five years, ten years, or even your whole life. But in a world where companies come and go—where they grow from nothing to the Fortune 500 and then disappear, all in a few years—that's just not possible.

Here's the deal, and here's what I told Doug: The time to

look for a new job is when you don't need one. The time to switch jobs is before it feels comfortable. Go. Switch. Challenge yourself; get yourself a raise and a promotion. You owe it to your career and your skills.

If your job is a Cul-de-Sac, you have to quit or accept the fact that your career is over.

Quitting Is Not the Same as Failing

Strategic quitting is a conscious decision you make based on the choices that are available to you. If you realize you're at a dead end compared with what you could be investing in, quitting is not only a reasonable choice, it's a smart one.

Failing, on the other hand, means that your dream is over. Failing happens when you give up, when there are no other options, or when you quit so often that you've used up all your time and resources.

It's easy to wring your hands about becoming a failure. Quitting smart, though, is a great way to avoid failing.

Coping Is a Lousy Alternative to Quitting

Coping is what people do when they try to muddle through. They cope with a bad job or a difficult task. The problem with coping is that it never leads to exceptional performance. Mediocre work is rarely because of a lack of talent and often because of the Cul-de-Sac. All coping does is waste your time and misdirect your energy. If the best you can do is cope, you're better off quitting.

Quitting is better than coping because quitting frees you up to excel at something else.

"Never Quit"

What a spectacularly bad piece of advice. It ranks up there with "Oh, that's a funny dirty joke, let's tell the teacher!" Never quit? Never quit wetting your bed? Or that job you had at Burger King in high school? Never quit selling a product that is now obsolete?

Wait a minute. Didn't that coach say quitting was a bad idea?

Actually, quitting as a short-term strategy is a bad idea. Quitting for the long term is an excellent idea.

I think the advice-giver meant to say, "Never quit something with great long-term potential just because you can't deal with the stress of the moment." Now *that's* good advice.

Pride Is the Enemy of the Smart Quitter

Richard Nixon sacrificed tens of thousands of innocent lives (on both sides) when he refused to quit the Vietnam war. The only reason he didn't quit sooner: pride. The very same pride that keeps someone in the same career years after it has become unattractive and no fun. The very same pride that keeps a restaurant open long after it's clear that business is just not going to pick up.

When you're facing a Cul-de-Sac, what's your reason for sticking? Are you too proud to quit?

One reason people feel really good after they quit a dead-end project is that they discover that hurting one's pride is not fatal. You work up the courage to quit, bracing yourself for the sound of your ego being ripped to shreds—and then everything is okay.

If pride is the only thing keeping you from quitting, if there's no Dip to get through, you're likely wasting an enormous amount of time and money defending something that will heal pretty quickly.

Harvard Medical School Is Not a Reason to Stick (Ignore Sunk Costs!)

Best-selling author Michael Crichton quit as he was on his way to a career at the top of his profession. When he gave up medicine, Crichton had already graduated from Harvard Medical School and done a postdoctoral fellowship study at the Salk Institute for Biological Studies, guaranteeing him a lucrative career as a doctor or as a researcher. He traded it for the unpredictable life of an author.

Crichton had no stomach for cutting people open, and he decided he didn't relish the future a medical career would bring him, regardless of how successful he might become at it. So he quit. Crichton saw that just because he had already gotten into Harvard, already earned a fellowship—already made it through the Dip—he didn't have to spend the rest of his life doing something he didn't enjoy in order to preserve his pride.

He stopped cold turkey and started over. If he can quit, can you?

Three Questions to Ask Before Quitting

If you're thinking about quitting (or not quitting), then you've succeeded. (And so have I.) Realizing that quitting is worth your focus and consideration is the first step to becoming the best in the world. The next step is to ask three questions.

QUESTION 1: AM I PANICKING?

Quitting is not the same as panicking. Panic is never premeditated. Panic attacks us, it grabs us, it is in the moment.

Quitting when you're panicked is dangerous and expensive. The best quitters, as we've seen, are the ones who *decide in advance* when they're going to quit. You can always quit later—so wait until you're done panicking to decide.

When the pressure is greatest to compromise, to drop out, or to settle, your desire to quit should be at its lowest. The decision to quit is often made in the moment. But that's exactly the wrong time to make such a critical decision. The reason so many of us quit in the Dip is that without a compass or a plan, the easiest thing to do is to give up. While that might be the easiest path, it's also the least successful one.

QUESTION 2: WHO AM I TRYING TO INFLUENCE?

Are you trying to succeed in a market? Get a job? Train a muscle?

If you're considering quitting, it's almost certainly because you're not being successful at your current attempt at influence. If you have called on a prospect a dozen times without success, you're frustrated and considering giving up. If you've got a boss who just won't let up, you're considering quitting your job. And if you're a marketer with a product that doesn't seem to be catching on, you're wondering if you should abandon this product and try another.

If you're trying to influence just one person, persistence has its limits. It's easy to cross the line between demonstrating your commitment and being a pest. If you haven't influenced him yet, it may very well be time to quit.

One person or organization will behave differently than a *market* of people will. One person has a particular agenda and a single worldview. One person will make up his mind and if you're going to succeed, you'll have to change it. And changing someone's mind is difficult, if not impossible.

If you're trying to influence a market, though, the rules are different. Sure, some of the people in a market have considered you (and even rejected you). But most of the people in the market have never even heard of you. The market doesn't have just one mind. Different people in the market are seeking different things.

Sergey Brin, cofounder of Google, told me, "We knew that Google was going to get better every single day as we worked on it, and we knew that sooner or later, everyone was going to try it. So our feeling was that the later you tried it, the better it was for us because we'd make a better impression with better technology. So we were never in a big hurry to get you to use it today. Tomorrow would be better."

Influencing one person is like scaling a wall. If you get over the wall the first few tries, you're in. If you don't, often you'll find that the wall gets higher with each attempt.

Influencing a market, on the other hand, is more of a hill than a wall. You can make progress, one step at a time, and as you get higher, it actually gets easier. People in the market talk to each other. They are influenced by each other. So every step of progress you make actually gets amplified.

QUESTION 3: WHAT SORT OF MEASURABLE PROGRESS AM I MAKING?

If you're trying to succeed in a job or a relationship or at a task, you're either moving forward, falling behind, or standing still. There are only three choices.

To succeed, to get to that light at the end of the tunnel, you've got to make some sort of forward progress, no matter how small. Too often, we get stuck in a situation where quitting seems too painful, so we just stay with it, choosing not to quit because it's easier than quitting. That choice—to stick with it in the absence of forward progress—is a waste. It's a waste because of the opportunity cost—you could be doing something far better, and far more pleasurable, with your time.

Measurable progress doesn't have to be a raise or a promotion. It can be more subtle than that, but it needs to be more than a mantra, more than just "surviving is succeeding." The challenge, then, is to surface new milestones in areas where you have previously expected to find none.

If you've got a small business and you are keeping a few customers happy, it's fine to keep on keeping on because, over time, those customers can get you new customers. You can measure your progress by referrals and sales growth. Your consistency and market presence, all by themselves, are enough to justify your efforts (sometimes). If, on the other hand, your business doesn't generate word of mouth, doesn't see new customers, and isn't moving forward, why exactly are you sticking with it?

When you are trying to influence an entire market, the value of not quitting is quite high. Yes, you should probably be eager to quit a marketing tactic that isn't paying for itself, or even a particular product feature that isn't appealing to your target audience. But your commitment to the market needs to be unquestioned—it's much cheaper and easier to build your foundation in one market than to flit from one to another until you find a quick success.

Let's slow down and think that through for a second. Quitting a job is not quitting your quest to make a living or a difference or an impact. Quitting a job doesn't have to mean giving up. A job is just a tactic, a way to get to what you really want. As soon as your job hits a dead end, it makes sense to quit and take your quest to a bigger marketplace—because every day you wait puts your goal further away.

The same is true for an organization. You don't define yourself by the tactics you use. Instead, your organization succeeds or fails in its efforts to reach its big goals. And the moment your tactics are no longer part of winning the Dip—the moment they are in a Cul-de-Sac—you are obligated to switch tactics at the same time you most definitely keep aiming for the bigger goal.

The seduction of not quitting—and the source of all

those stories about sticking it out—almost always comes from people moving *through* a market. When you hear about an author who got turned down thirty times before signing with a publisher or of an overnight sensation who paid her dues for a decade in coffee shops, you're seeing how persistence pays off *across* a market.

On the other hand, when was the last time you heard about someone who stuck with a dead-end job or a dead-end relationship or a dead-end sales prospect until suddenly, one day, the person at the other end said, "Wow, I really admire your persistence; let's change our relationship for the better"? It doesn't happen.

Quitting Before You Start

Here's an assignment for you: Write it down. Write down under what circumstances you're willing to quit. And when. And then stick with it.

Deciding in Advance When to Quit

Here's a quote from ultramarathoner Dick Collins:

> Decide before the race the conditions that will cause you to stop and drop out. You don't want to be out there saying, "Well gee, my leg hurts, I'm a little dehydrated,

I'm sleepy, I'm tired, and it's cold and windy." And talk yourself into quitting. If you are making a decision based on how you feel at that moment, you will probably make the wrong decision.

So, there's tool number one. If quitting is going to be a strategic decision that enables you to make smart choices in the marketplace, then you should outline your quitting strategy *before* the discomfort sets in.

Just as a smart venture capitalist pressures the board of directors to have a plan in case they run out of money, every individual and every organization that wants to use quitting as a competitive tool ought to have a plan about when it's time to quit.

If quitting in the face of the Dip is a bad idea, then quitting when you're facing a Cul-de-Sac is a great idea. The hard part is having the perspective to see this when you're in pain, or frustrated, or stuck. That's why setting your limits *before* you start is so powerful.

Soft Tires . . . Pick Your Dip

Consider the bicycle tire.

The first ten pounds of pressure you put into a completely flat tire do no good at all. And adding ten *extra* pounds to a full tire will burst the tire, defeating the entire purpose of your effort. No, it's just the last ten pounds, the ones that get it to full that really pay off.

When it's down five or ten pounds, it might as well be flat. A 10-percent change in pressure makes it defective. If it's up five or ten pounds, though, the entire wheel is threatened with a blowout. Obviously, it's the pressure right around full that has the most impact.

If you enter a market that's too big or too loud for the amount of resources you have available, your message is going to get lost. Your marketing disappears, your message fails to spread. Think twice before launching a mass-market brand of chewing gum. Like adding just a few pounds of air to a flat tire, launching a product into too big of a market has little effect. You can't create pressure and you never reach the Dip.

When Sara Lee tried to enter the market for home coffee machines and pods with their Senseo coffeemaker, they didn't have enough resources to get through the Dip . . . not in the United States, anyway.

In the Netherlands, a much smaller market, Senseo has reached a 40-percent market share of all households. They have the right amount of pressure for the "tire" that is that (tiny) market. In the United States, on the other hand, they report that only 1 percent of households have a Senseo. Too big a market, too few resources. Stuck in the Dip.

Since few Americans have a Senseo, few talk about it. Few stores promote the pods. The word doesn't spread and Senseo can't reach critical mass—there are too many places for the message to go and not enough resources to get it there.

Figure out how much pressure you've got available, *then* pick your tire. Not too big, not too small.

You're Astonishing

How dare you waste it.

You and your organization have the power to change everything. To create remarkable products and services. To over deliver. To be the best in the world.

How dare you squander that resource by spreading it too thin.

How dare you settle for mediocre just because you're busy coping with too many things on your agenda, racing against the clock to get it all done.

The lesson is simple: If you've got as much as you've got, use it. Use it to become the best in the world, to change the game, to set the agenda for everyone else. You can only do that by marshaling all of your resources to get through the biggest possible Dip. In order to get through that Dip, you'll need to quit everything else. If it's not going to put a dent in the world, quit. Right now. Quit and use that void to find the energy to assault the Dip that matters.

Go ahead, make something happen. We're waiting!

Questions

Is this a Dip, a Cliff, or a Cul-de-Sac?

If it's a Cul-de-Sac, how can I change it into a Dip?

Is my persistence going to pay off in the long run?

Am I engaged with just one person (or organization), or do my actions in this situation spill over into the entire marketplace?

When should I quit? I need to decide now, not when I'm in the middle of it, and not when part of me is begging to quit.

If I quit this task, will it increase my ability to get through the Dip on something more important?

If I'm going to quit anyway, is there something dramatic I can do instead that might change the game?

Should I really be calling on IBM? Should I really be trying to get on *Oprah*?

What chance does this project have to be the best in the world?

Who decides what *best* is?

Can we make the *world* smaller?

Does it make sense to submit a résumé to every single ad on Craigslist, just to see what happens?

If I like my job, is it time to quit?

Is doing nothing better than planning on quitting and then doing something great?

Are you avoiding the remarkable as a way of quitting without quitting?

If it scares you, it might be a good thing to try.

The Best in the World?

The best in the world? Sripraphai, Hard Manufacturing, Toyota Prius, JetBlue, Gulfstream, Nordost, Kate's Paperie, Peet's, Silpat, Robin Dellabough, Starbucks, iPod, Jackson Pollock, Allison Sweet, Paychex, Sotheby's, Porsche, Barry Diller, Megan Casey, Helene Godin, Paul Graham, Google, White Stripes, Red Maxwell, Terry Gross, Tony Hawk, Heinz Ketchup, Shaun White, Catherine E. Oliver, iStockphoto. com, Leica, Jonathan Sackner Bernstein, Lark, Chubb, SmartGlove, Beckham, Madonna, Elvis, Boing Boing, the Three Stooges, Ben Zander, Stephen King, Amazon.com, Hood River Gorge, Sundance, CBGB, Paris (the city, not the person), Denny's, Lisa DiMona, Johnny Cash, Mia Hamm, Michael Jordan, Rolex, Serious Strengths, the Empire State Building, Hugh Macleod, CAA, Will Weisser, Bob Dylan, *Dilbert*, *Doonesbury*, De Cecco pasta, FedEx, Momofuku, Adrian Zackheim, *The New Yorker*, Burgerville, Coach, the

Eiffel Tower, Gil Hildebrand, Jr., Tesla Motors, Lynn Gordon, Corey Brown, Swan, WD 40, Mo & Alex, Scharffen Berger, Anne Shepherd, Chestnut Canoe, Ideo, Tom Demott, Poilane, *Casablanca*, Amoeba Records, Charlotte Okie, the Tattered Cover, Jennifer Young, Joseph Perez, Miles Davis, Crooked Brook, and Marilyn Wishnie.

Acknowledgments

This book is really short. Short books are hard to write, but you made me do it. My readers are excellent correspondents, and this is something I've learned from them along the way: Write less.

It's Almost Impossible to Overinvest in Becoming the Market Leader.

All our successes are the same. All our failures, too.

We succeed when we do something remarkable.

We fail when we give up too soon.

We succeed when we are the best in the world at what we do.

We fail when we get distracted by tasks we don't have the guts to quit.

Share the Dip

Who else is stuck? Make a list of co-workers who need to learn about quitting and then circulate this book when you're done. Add a few names, then pass it on (cross yourself off the list before you do).

_____

_____

_____

_____

_____

_____

_____

_____

Please return this to: _____

If you've enjoyed *The Dip*, check out these other thought-provoking, bestselling books by Seth Godin:

All Marketers Are Liars

Free Prize Inside!

Linchpin

Permission Marketing

Poke the Box

Purple Cow

Small Is the New Big

This Is Marketing

Tribes

Unleashing the Ideavirus

Visit www.SethGodin.com for more information . . . and click on Seth's head to read his blog.